IT'S TIME TO EAT BLACK BEANS

It's Time to Eat
BLACK BEANS

Walter the Educator

Silent King Books
A WhichHead Entertainment Imprint

Copyright © 2024 by Walter the Educator

All rights reserved. No part of this book may be reproduced in any manner whatsoever without written per- mission except in the case of brief quotations embodied in critical articles and reviews.

First Printing, 2024

Disclaimer

This book is a literary work; the story is not about specific persons, locations, situations, and/or circumstances unless mentioned in a historical context. Any resemblance to real persons, locations, situations, and/or circumstances is coincidental. This book is for entertainment and informational purposes only. The author and publisher offer this information without warranties expressed or implied. No matter the grounds, neither the author nor the publisher will be accountable for any losses, injuries, or other damages caused by the reader's use of this book. The use of this book acknowledges an understanding and acceptance of this disclaimer.

It's Time to Eat BLACK BEANS is a collectible early learning book by Walter the Educator suitable for all ages belonging to Walter the Educator's Time to Eat Book Series. Collect more books at WaltertheEducator.com

USE THE EXTRA SPACE TO TAKE NOTES AND DOCUMENT YOUR MEMORIES

BLACK BEANS

It's time to eat, oh what a treat,

It's Time to Eat
Black Beans

Black beans are tasty, can't be beat!

In a little bowl or on some rice,

Warm and yummy, oh so nice.

Black beans are soft, they're small and round,

When they're cooked, they make a sound!

A little bubble, a steamy hiss,

A pot of beans is full of bliss.

With a sprinkle of salt and maybe some spice,

They're good with tacos, so very nice.

Add some veggies, a little cheese,

Black beans can please with ease.

They come from farms where the sun shines bright,

Grown in the ground, they're quite a sight.

Farmers pick them, wash them clean,

And now they're ready, black beans supreme!

It's Time to Eat
Black Beans

Spoon in hand, take a bite,

Black beans make your tummy feel right.

They give you strength to run and play,

To jump and laugh the whole long day.

Mix them with corn or avocado,

Or roll them up in a little burrito.

Put them in soup or eat them plain,

Black beans are never boring or lame!

They're full of goodness, that's a fact,

Protein and fiber, all neatly packed.

For growing big and staying strong,

Black beans help you all day long.

Black beans are fun to share with friends,

A bowl of love that never ends.

Pass them around, the joy will spread,

It's Time to Eat Black Beans

With beans, your heart and soul are fed.

So let's say thank you to this bean so fine,

It's healthy and tasty every time!

Scoop them up and take a bite,

Black beans make everything feel just right.

Now sing it loud, let's all agree,

Black beans are the best for you and me!

Time to eat, let's dig right in,

It's Time to Eat Black Beans

Black beans for the win-win-win!

ABOUT THE CREATOR

Walter the Educator is one of the pseudonyms for Walter Anderson. Formally educated in Chemistry, Business, and Education, he is an educator, an author, a diverse entrepreneur, and he is the son of a disabled war veteran. "Walter the Educator" shares his time between educating and creating. He holds interests and owns several creative projects that entertain, enlighten, enhance, and educate, hoping to inspire and motivate you. Follow, find new works, and stay up to date with Walter the Educator™

at WaltertheEducator.com

www.ingramcontent.com/pod-product-compliance
Lightning Source LLC
LaVergne TN
LVHW052010060526
838201LV00059B/3959